ALSO BY TOMI UNGERER

The Underground Sketchbook

Tomi Ungerer's
Compromises

The Bodley Head • London

© Tomi Ungerer 1970
ISBN 0 370 01336 0
Printed in the United States of America for
The Bodley Head Ltd.
9 Bow Street, London, WC2
First published in Great Britain 1970

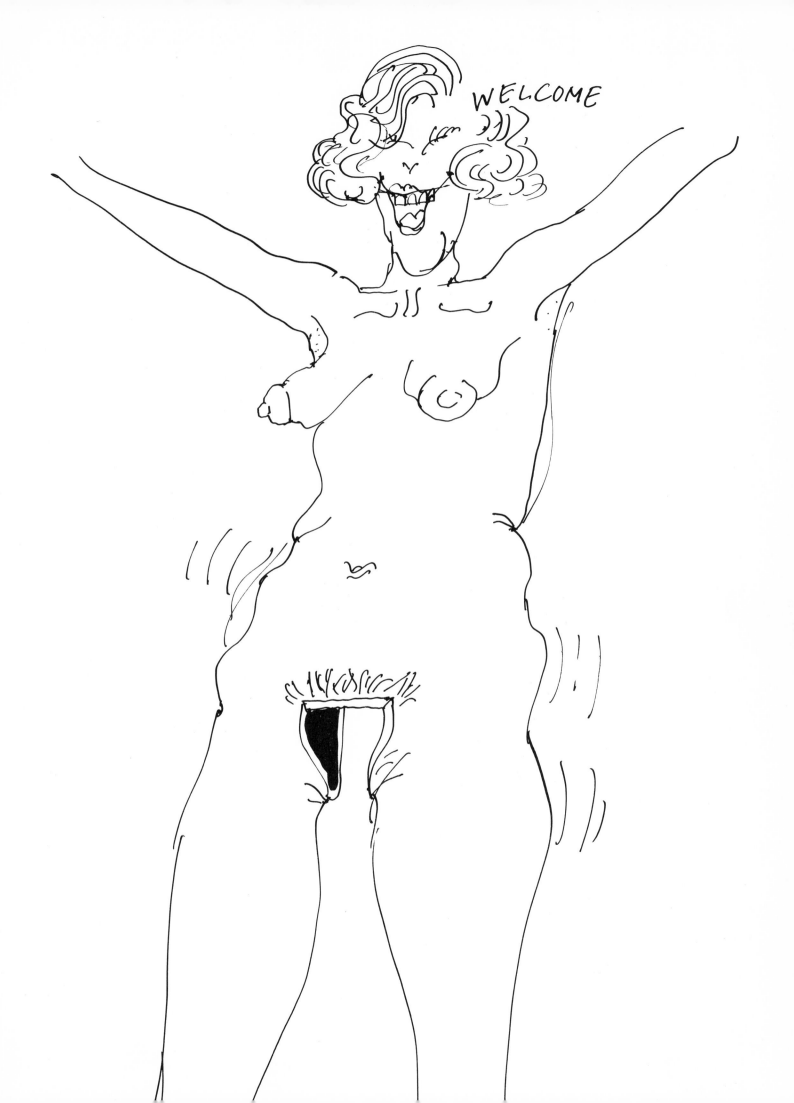

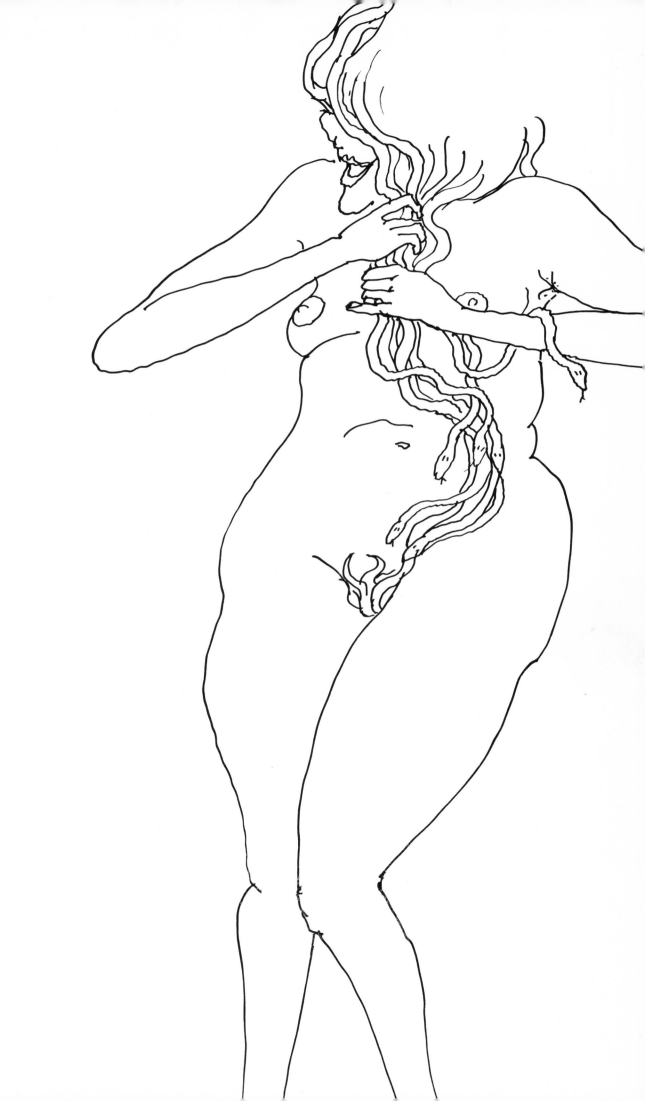

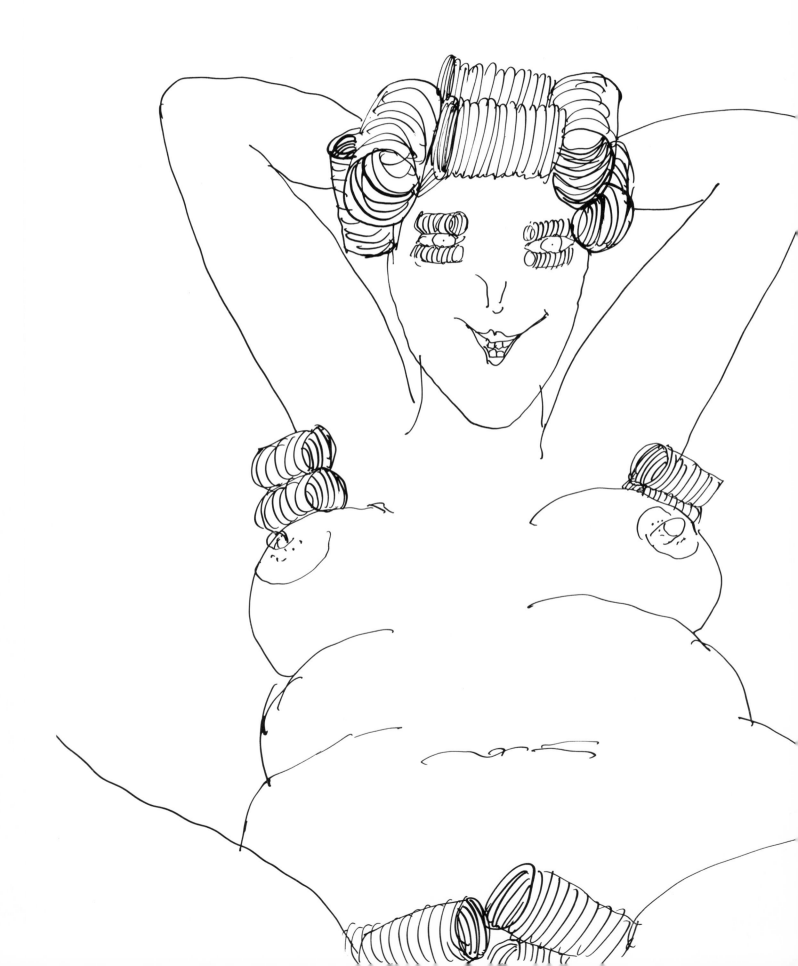

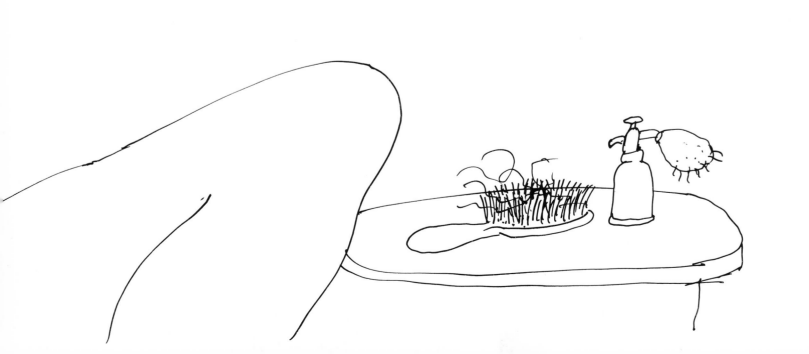

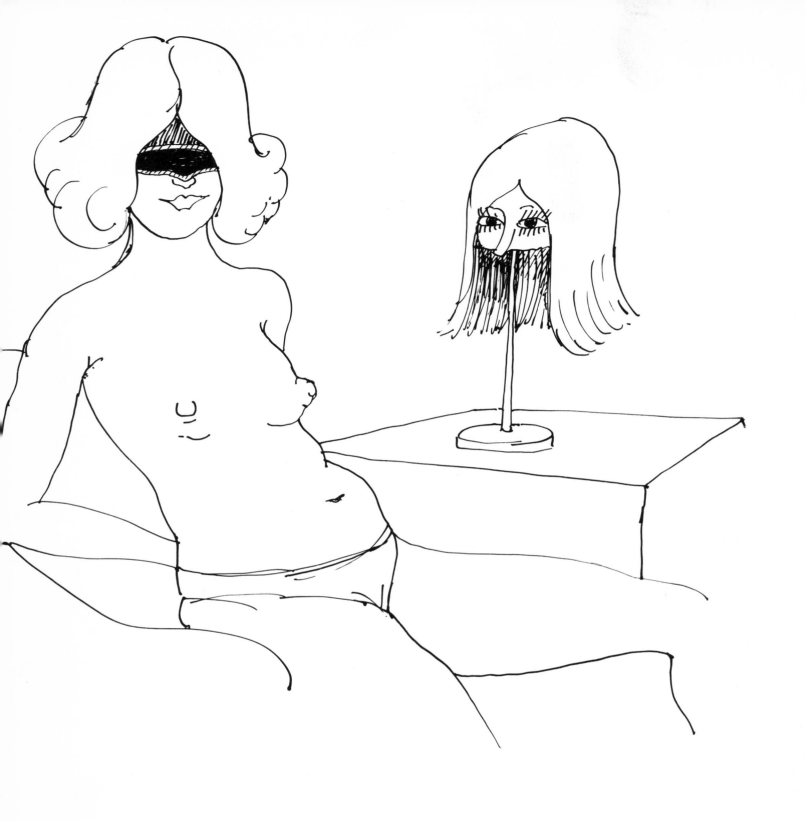

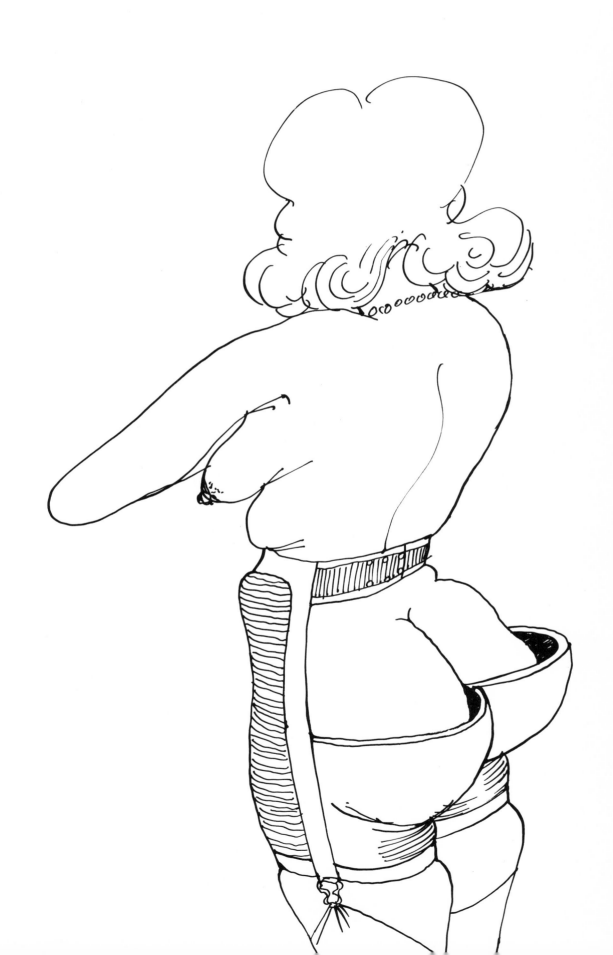

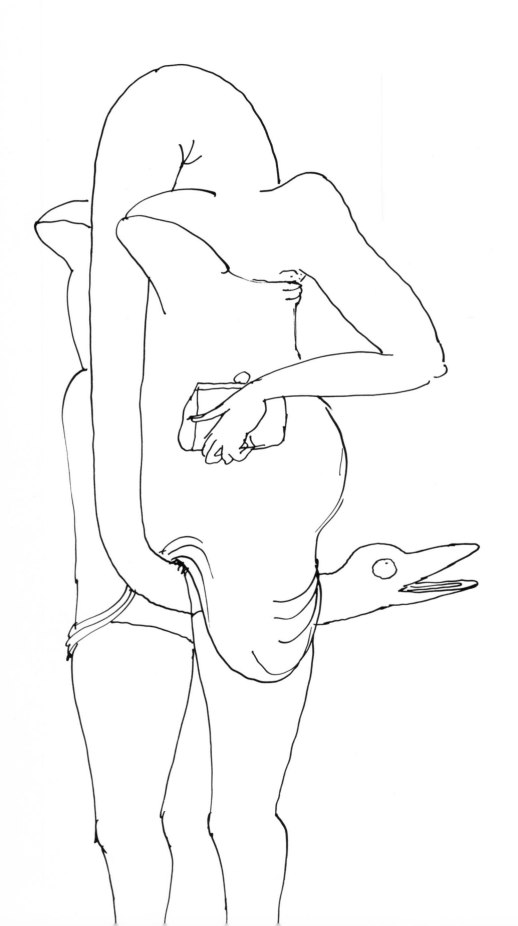

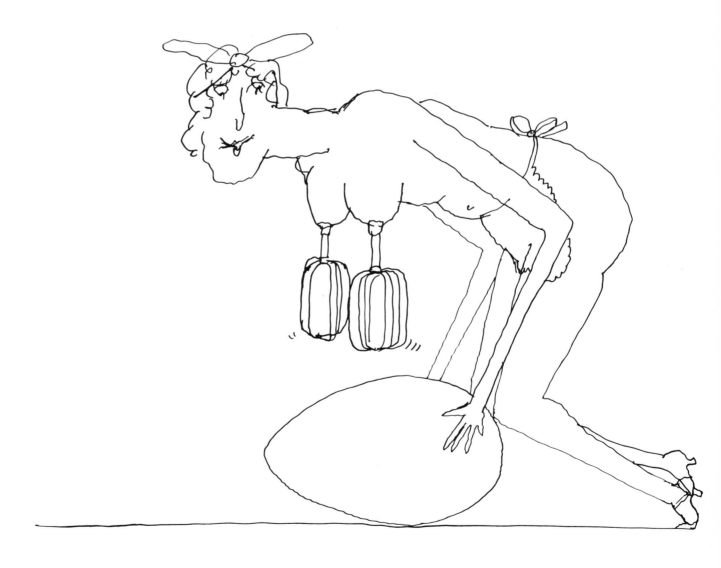

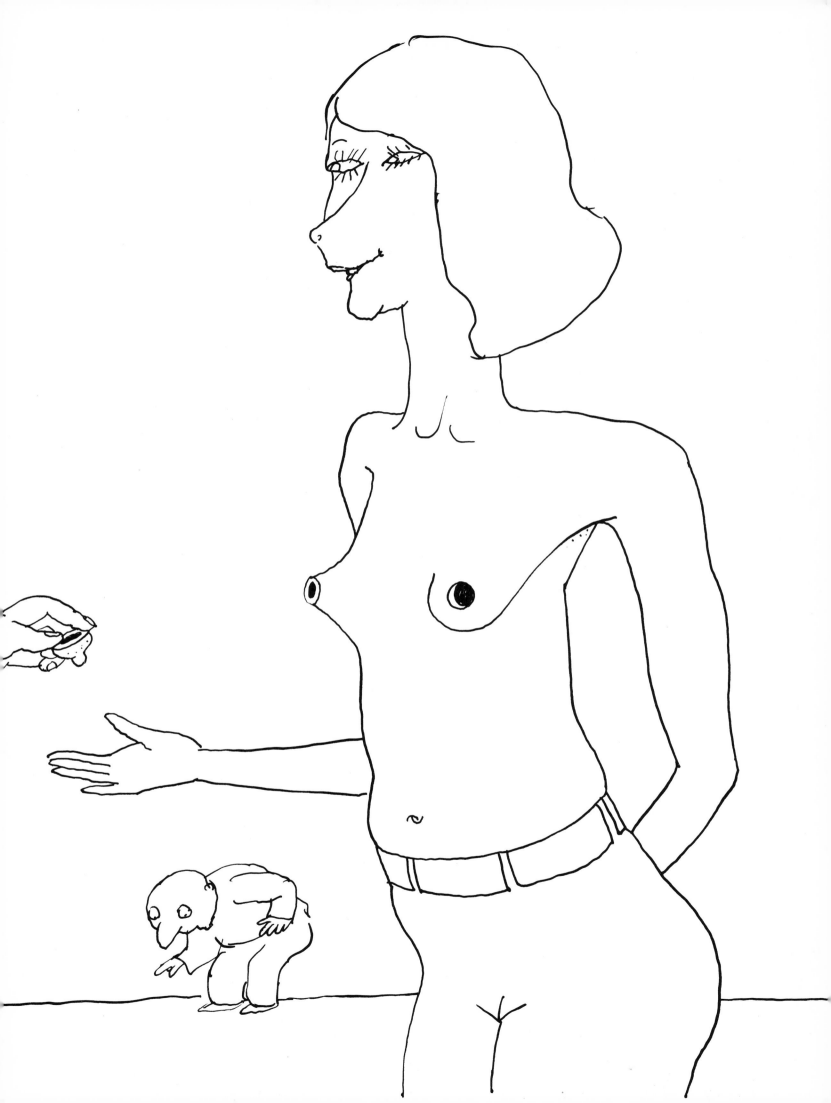

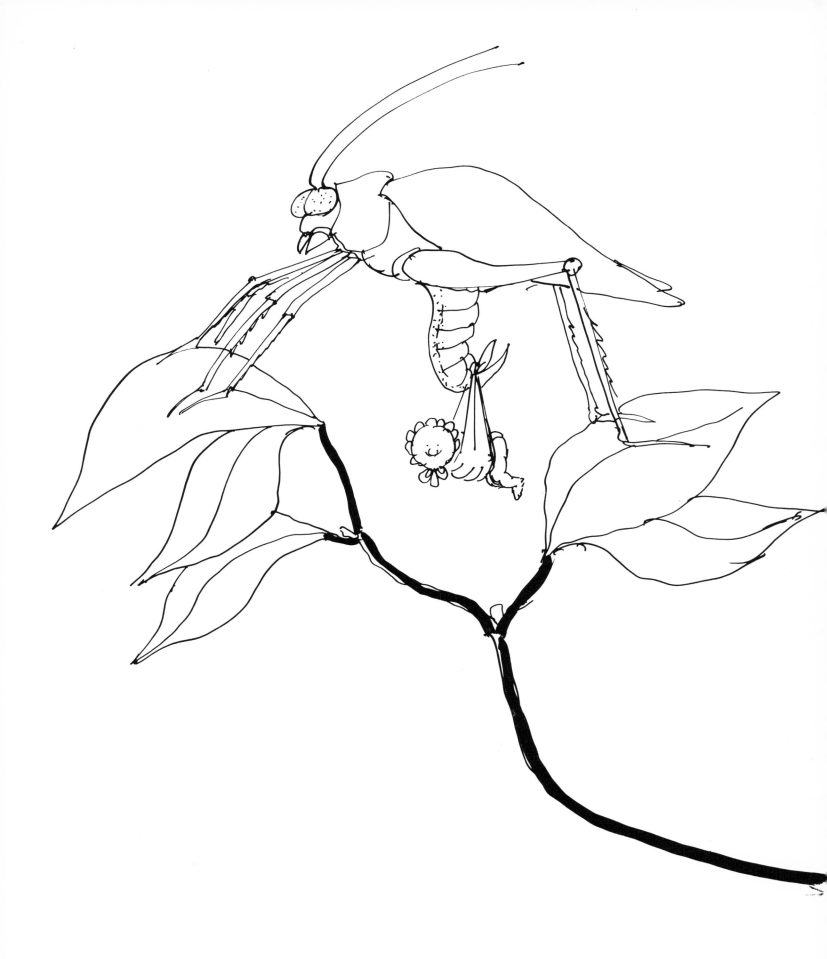

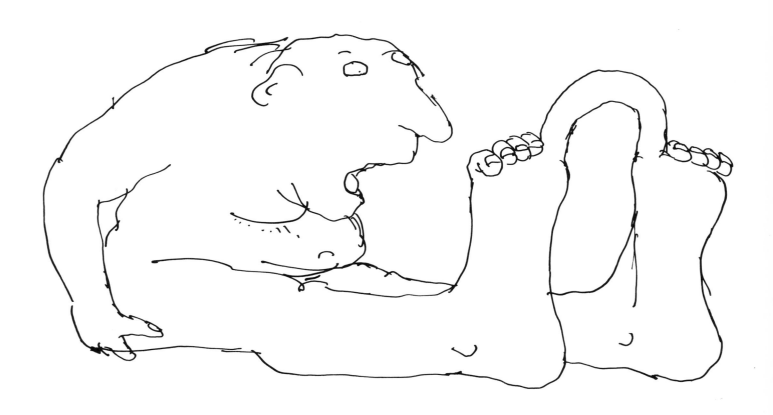

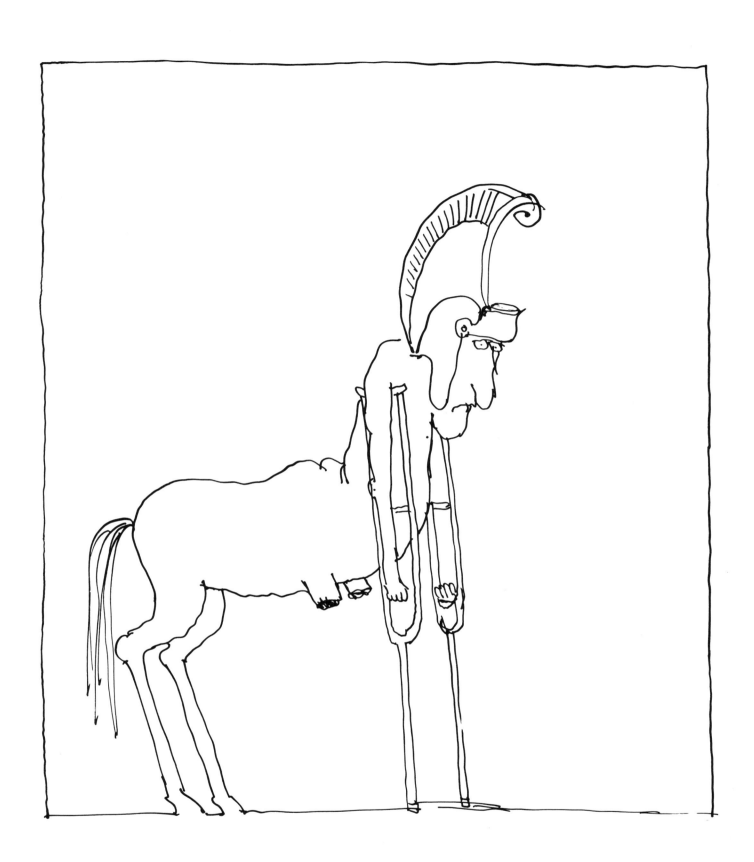

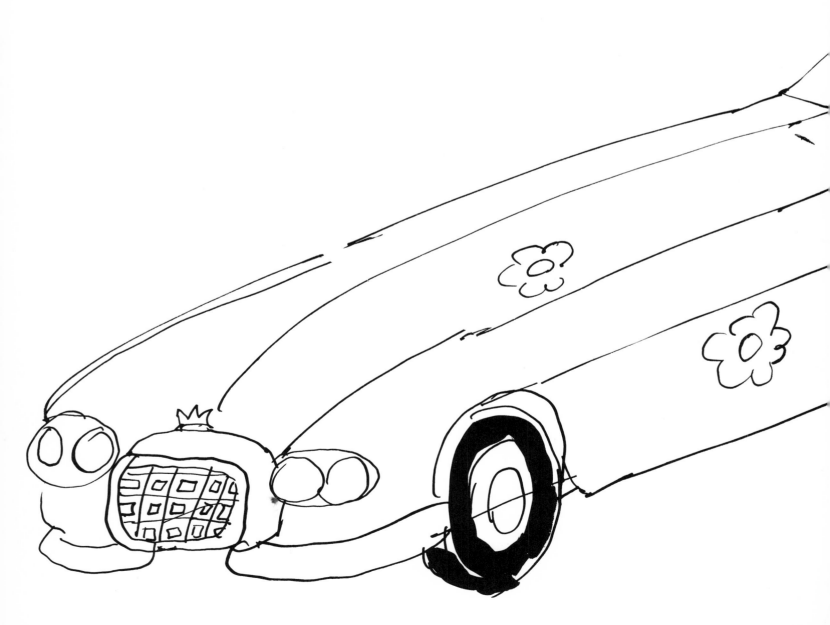

the new left

LEFT WING

PS

RIGHT WING

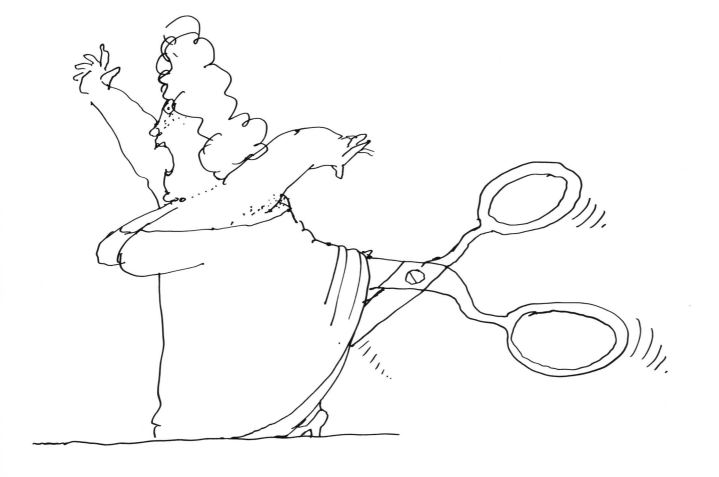

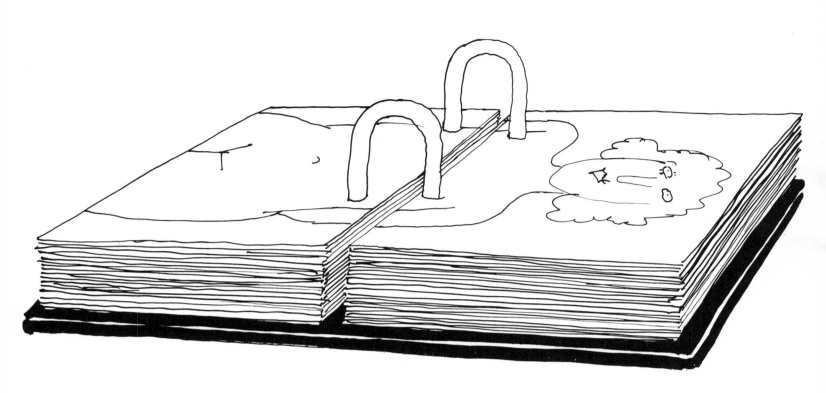

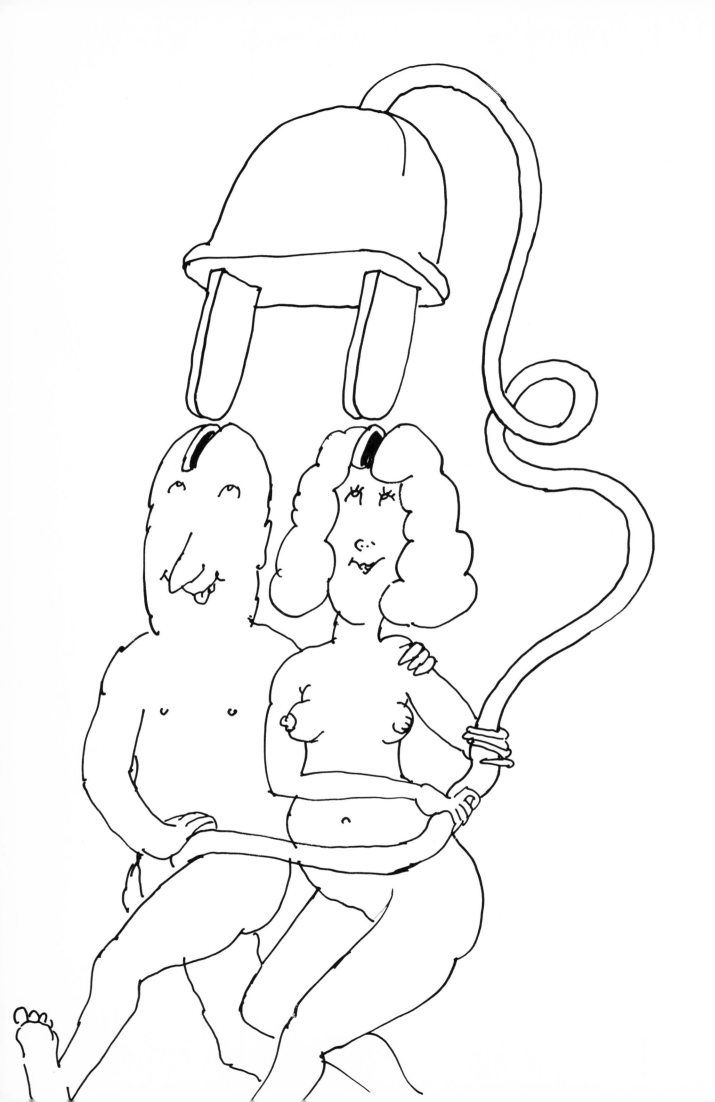

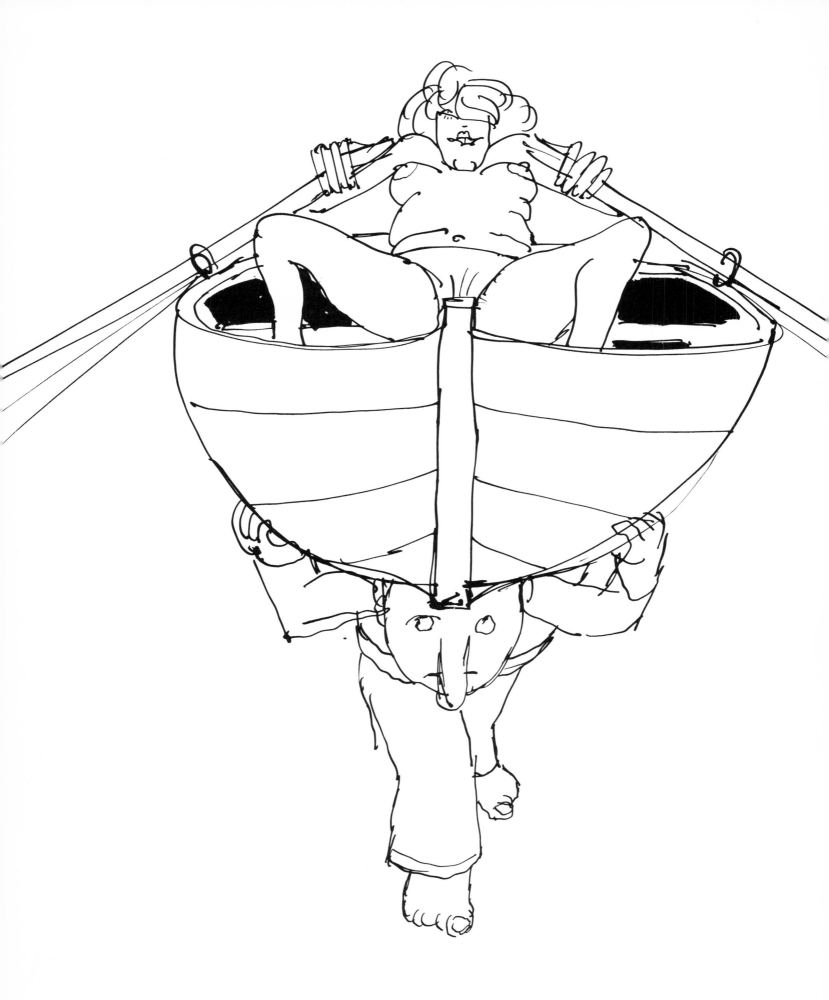

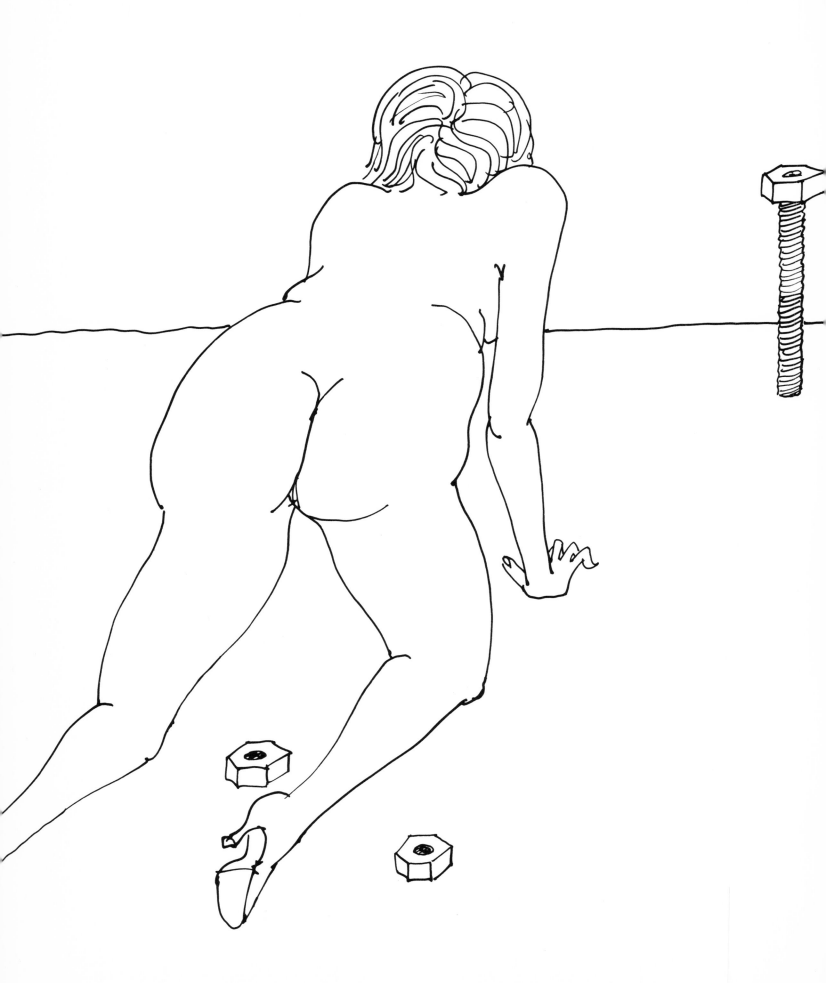

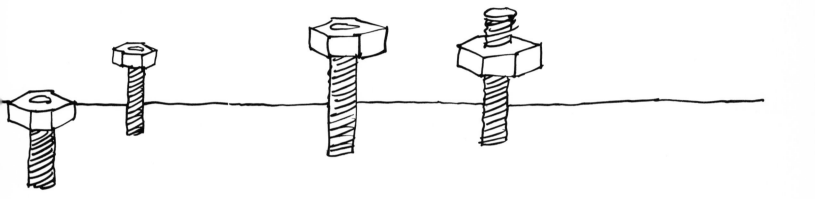

LOVE ME   LOVE ME NOT

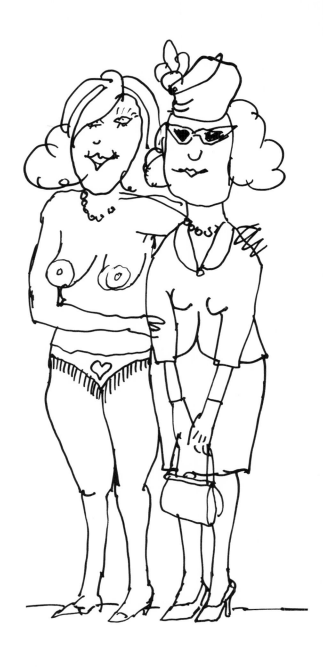

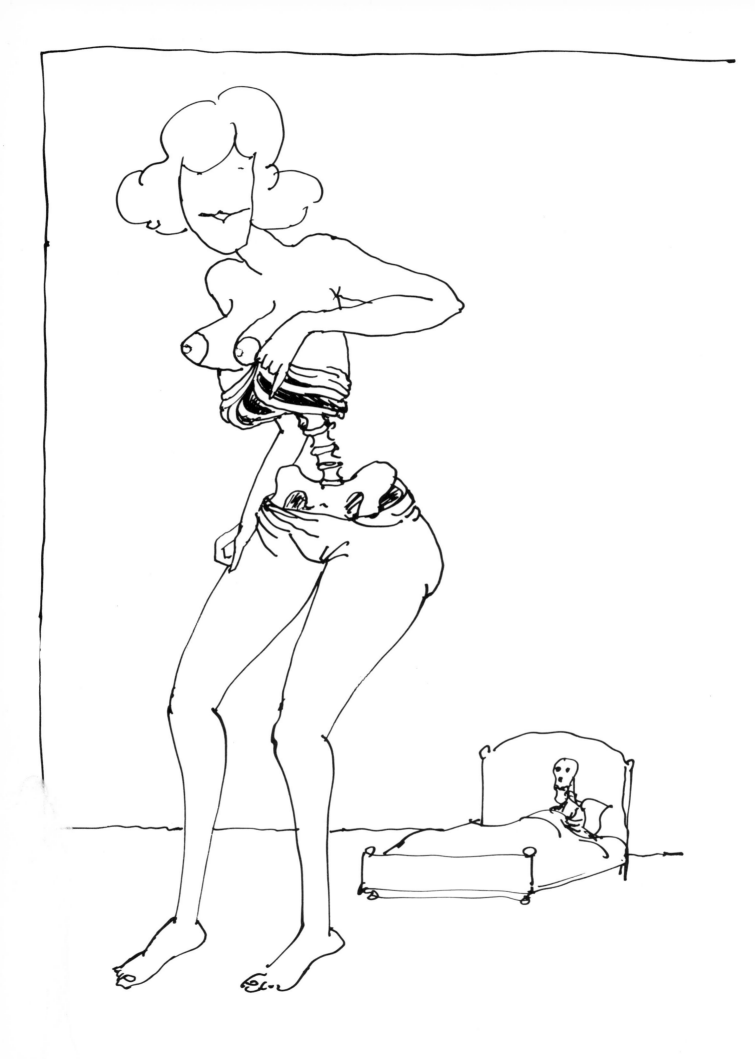

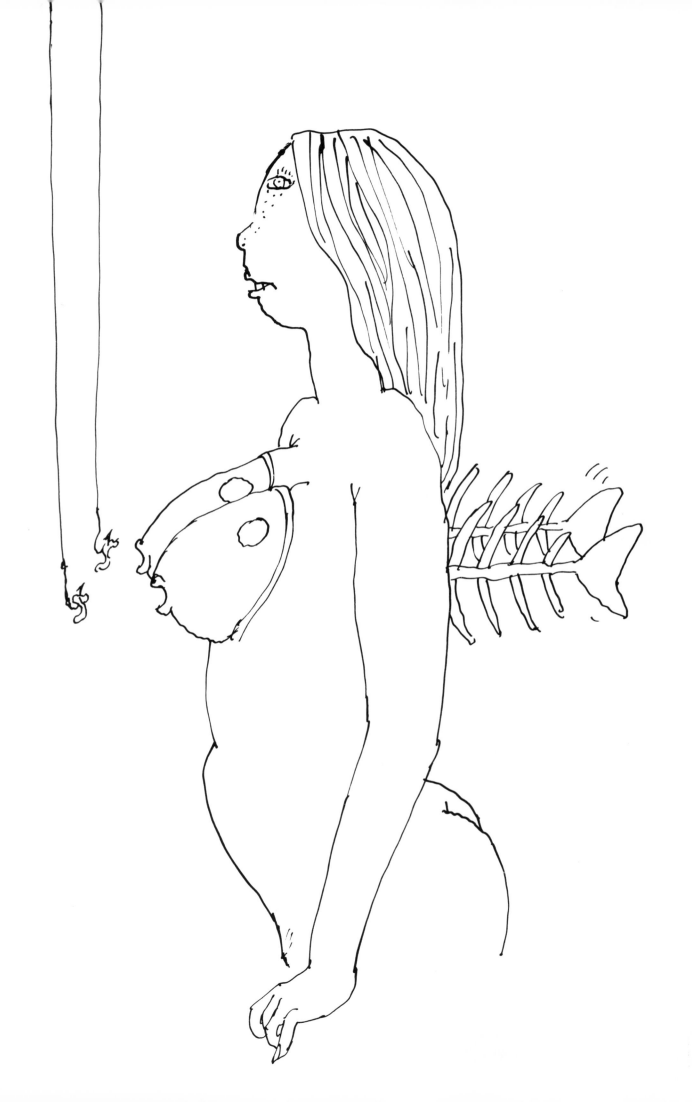

crack of dawn

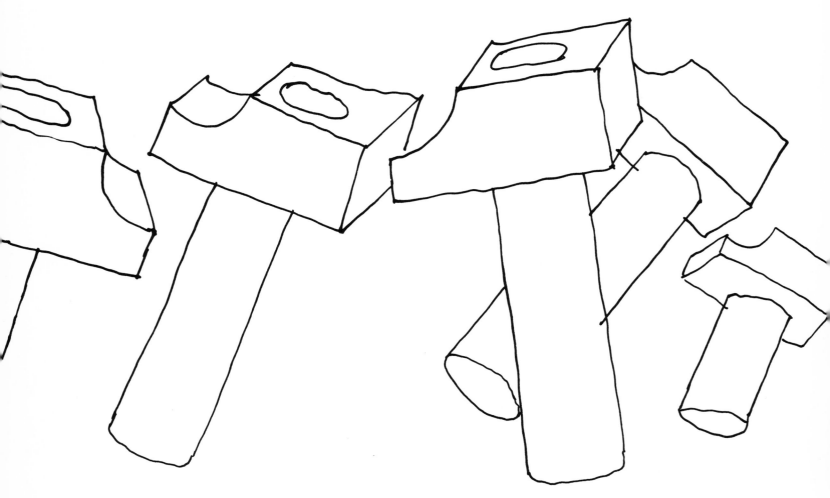

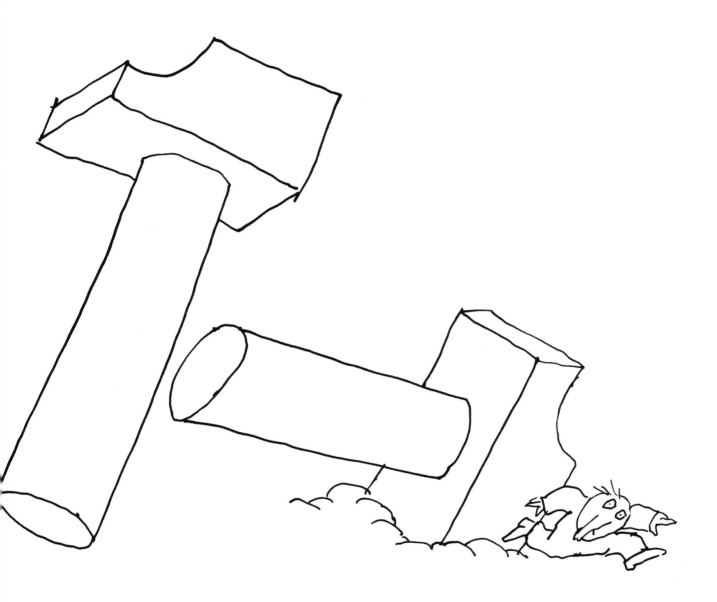

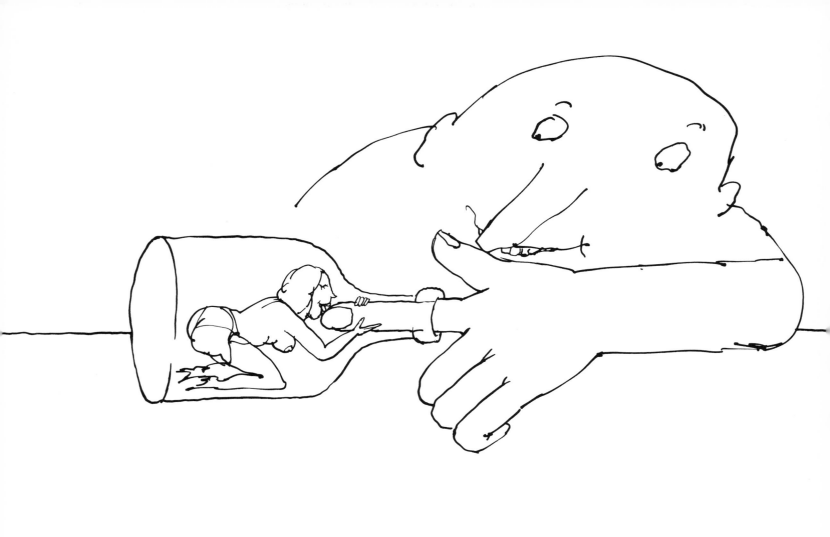

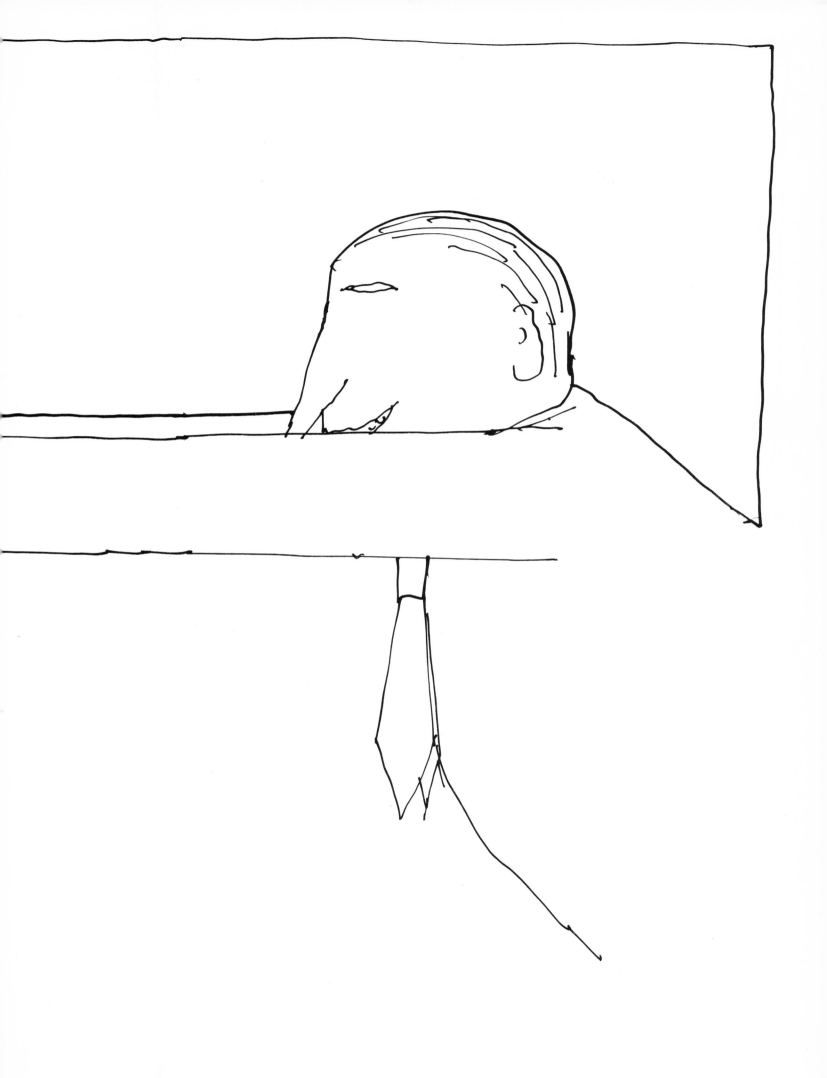

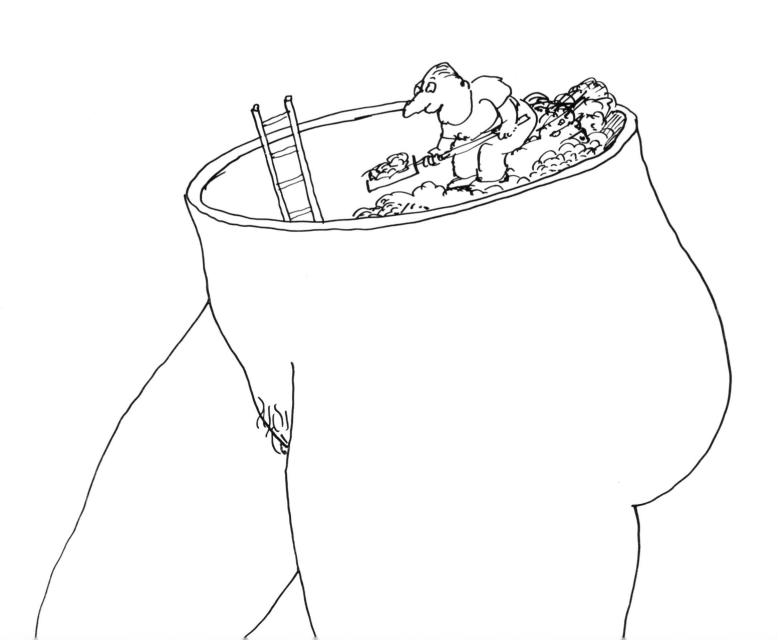

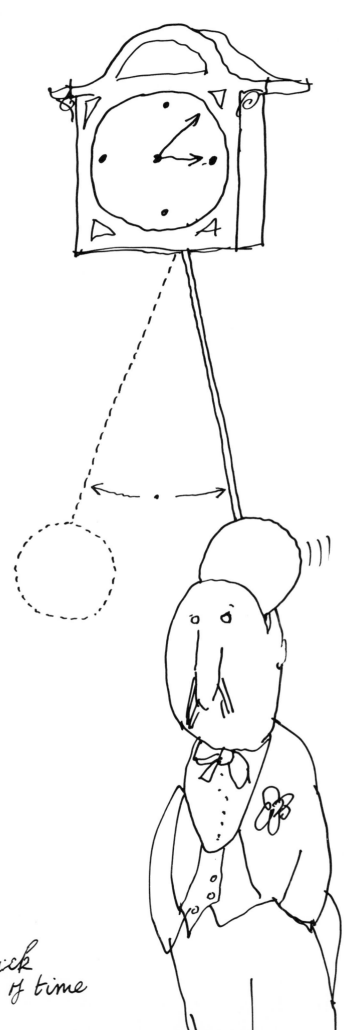

a nick
of time

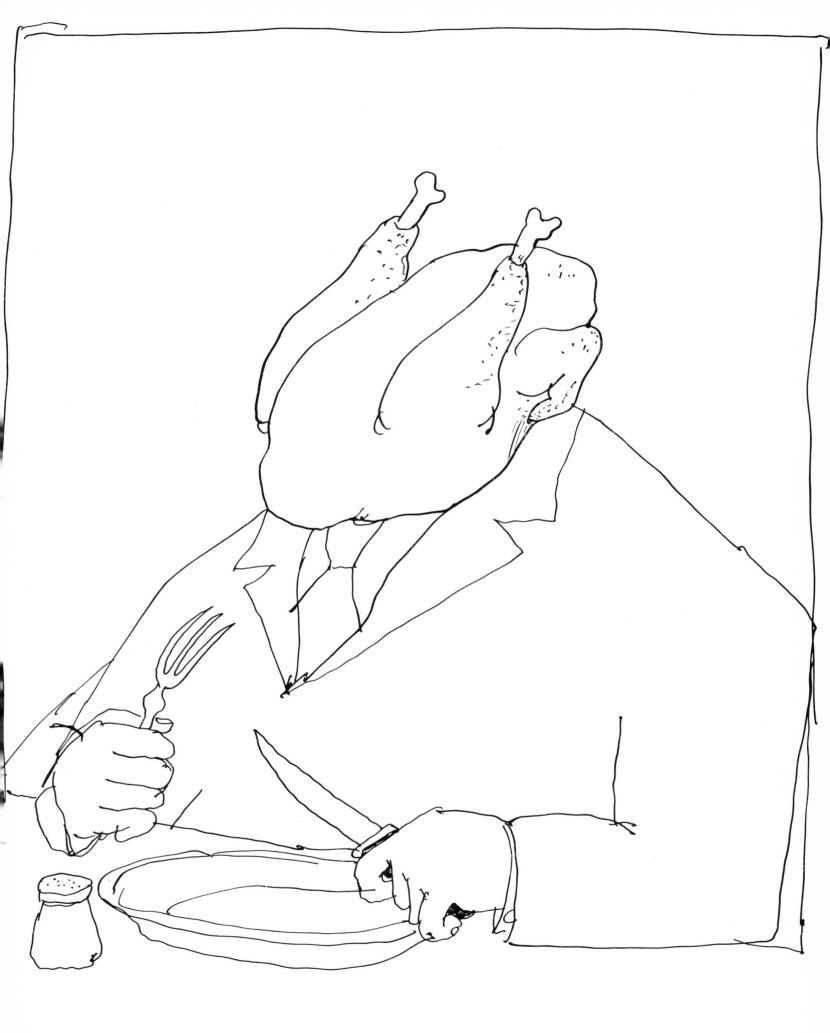

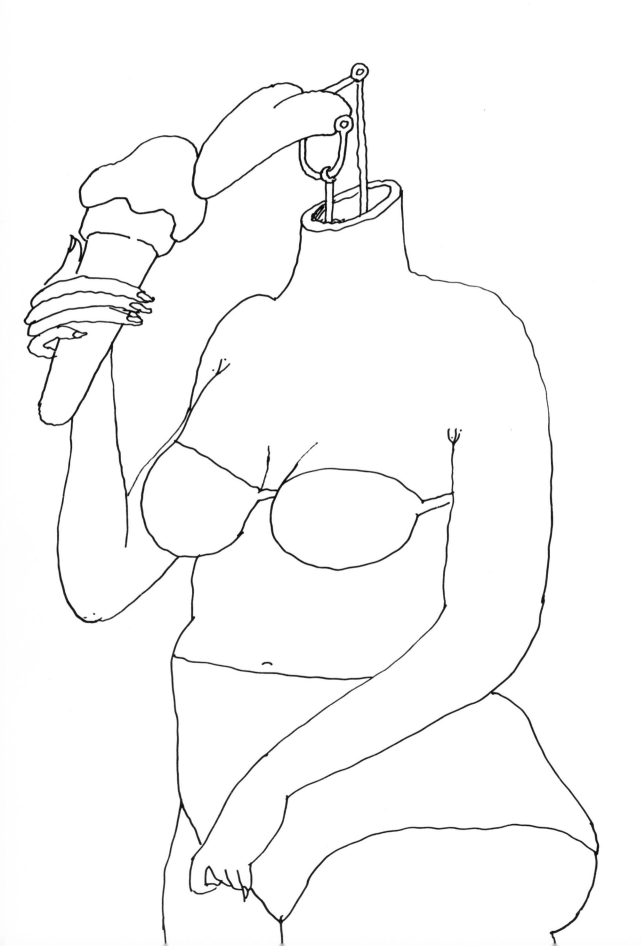

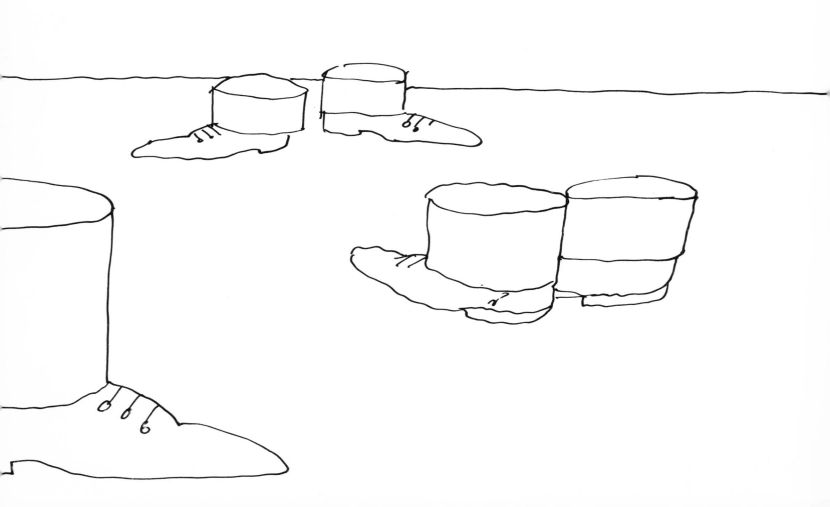

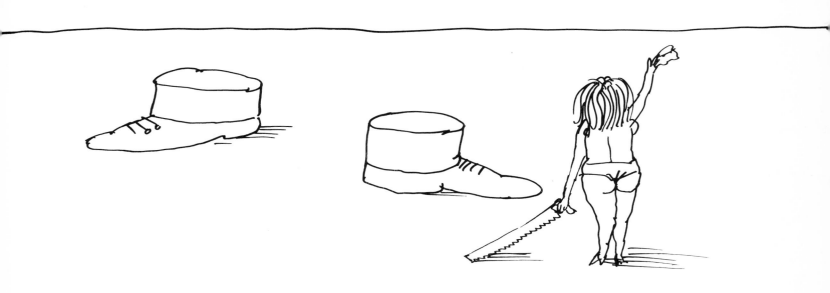